LITTLE BIG HEROES

A Handbook on the Tiny Creatures That Keep Our World Going

Hoe Yeen Nie

Illustrated by **David Liew**

Marshall Cavendish Children

Change Makers was created with Hwee Goh
who continues to provide oversight for this series.

© 2021 Marshall Cavendish International (Asia) Pte Ltd
Text © Hoe Yeen Nie
Illustrations © David Liew

Published by Marshall Cavendish Children
An imprint of Marshall Cavendish International

A member of the
Times Publishing Group

Other Marshall Cavendish Offices:
Marshall Cavendish Corporation, 800 Westchester Ave, Suite N-641, Rye
Brook, NY 10573, USA • Marshall Cavendish International (Thailand) Co Ltd,
253 Asoke, 16th Flr, Sukhumvit 21 Road, Klongtoey Nua, Wattana, Bangkok
10110, Thailand • Marshall Cavendish (Malaysia) Sdn Bhd, Times Subang,
Lot 46, Subang Hi-Tech Industrial Park, Batu Tiga, 40000 Shah Alam,
Selangor Darul Ehsan, Malaysia

Marshall Cavendish is a registered trademark of Times Publishing Limited

National Library Board, Singapore Cataloguing in Publication Data

Name(s): Hoe, Yeen Nie, author. | Liew, David, illustrator.
Title: Little big heroes : a handbook on the tiny creatures that keep our
world going / Hoe Yeen Nie ; illustrated by David Liew.
Other Title(s): Handbook on the tiny creatures that keep our world going |
Change makers (Marshall Cavendish Children)
Description: Singapore : Marshall Cavendish Children, [2021]
Identifier(s): ISBN 978-981-4928-23-6 (hardcover)
Subject(s): LCSH: Microbiology--Juvenile literature. | Microorganisms--
Juvenile literature.
Classification: DDC 579--dc23

Printed in Singapore

CONTENTS

FIRST ENCOUNTERS OF THE WEIRD KIND

As early as 8,000 years ago, humans have suspected that microorganisms exist. But it was only in the 1670s that **microbes** were seen for the very first time. This sparked a scientific revolution and a whole new way of understanding our natural world.

What's That?
Microbes are tiny organisms such as bacteria. Many consist of just one cell. They are found nearly everywhere — from the Poles to the Equator, to deserts, the bottom of the sea and even inside volcanoes!

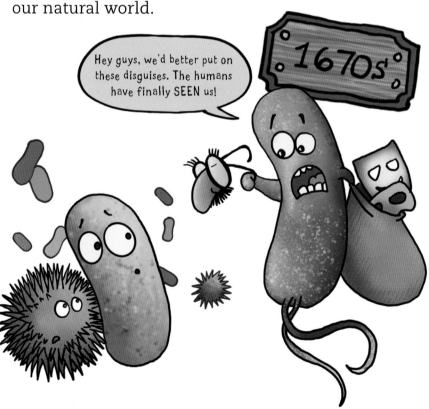

1670s

Hey guys, we'd better put on these disguises. The humans have finally SEEN us!

Hello Animalcules

In 1676, Dutchman Antonie van Leeuwenhoek scrapes some dental plaque from his teeth, places it under a microscope and peers into it. Whoa! What a strange sight! There were tiny creatures wriggling about, as if they were alive. Fascinated, van Leeuwenhoek calls them *animalcules* or "little animals". No one realised it then, but he had just discovered bacteria.

The Unlikely Scientist

For years, van Leeuwenhoek tries to convince Europe's top scientists of his discoveries. Few believe him. After all, he is a fabric merchant, not a trained scientist! But today van Leeuwenhoek is recognised as the pioneer of microbiology — the study of bacteria and other microorganisms.

I Spy with My Little Eye

Magnifying lenses have been in use for a long time, for instance to start fires. But it wasn't until the 1590s that a father-son team of spectacle makers in Holland invented what we now know as the microscope. This new instrument made tiny objects appear up to 300 times bigger, revealing details too small for the naked eye.

Did You Know?

In 1609, the Italian astronomer Galileo Galilei built his own microscope, which he called *occhiolino* or "little eye". But he soon switches attention to telescopes, aiming them at the night sky.

Did You Know?

Modern microscopes are now so powerful, they magnify objects to a million times and let us inspect cancer cells and even single atoms!

The Kitchen Aid

Humans have been making use of microbes for thousands of years, long before we could see them. Bread, kimchi, soy sauce, yoghurt, cheese and alcohol are made possible only by fermentation. That's the process in which bacteria, yeast and other microorganisms cause a chemical change in food and drink. We ferment food to preserve them or to improve their flavour.

MOBILE MICROBES

IT DOESN'T SMELL FUNNY IT'S FERMENTED!!

BIOFUEL!

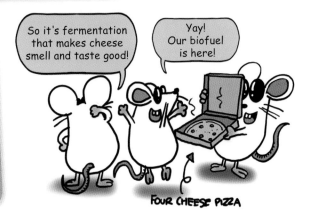

So it's fermentation that makes cheese smell and taste good!

Yay! Our biofuel is here!

FOUR CHEESE PIZZA

*See Change Makers: The Earth Experiment

Vampire Busters

Microbiology has helped us solve some of our biggest medical mysteries. One of them is tuberculosis (TB), an ancient and highly contagious lung disease. TB gave you a horrible fever, made you cough up blood and usually killed you. No wonder some thought it was caused by vampires! But in 1882, German scientist Robert Koch finally identified the bacteria responsible. In an era where TB killed one out of seven people in the US and Europe, his discovery was the most important step towards stopping the deadly disease.

Did You Know?

People once thought that bad air made them sick or spoiled their food. In the 1850s, French microbiologist Louis Pasteur proved the cause was *bacteria.

*See Change Makers: Invisible Enemies

TB has nothing to do with me, okay? Anyway, I need you to keep your blood INSIDE you. If you cough it up, there'll be nothing left for me!

Telescope borrowed from Galileo on page 6

Did you know that the German word for bat is "Fledermaus"? It means "flutter mouse"!

More Microbe Than Human

It might sound hard to believe, but the human body contains an entire world of microbes: bacteria, viruses, fungi and other microorganisms. It is estimated that the average adult has 30 trillion human cells and 39 trillion bacteria. In other words, only 43 per cent of our cells are human cells. That makes us more microbe than human!

Did You Know?

In 2015, researchers at the University of Cambridge, UK, revealed that human DNA contains genes from bacteria! They think this is a natural part of evolution.

Microbe CSI

Our **microbiome** is like a unique fingerprint. No two people, not even identical twins, have the same collection of microbes. It all depends on factors like where we live, what we eat and our health. This uniqueness is extremely useful for forensic researchers, who are investigating ways to use our microbiome to identify crime suspects or to determine how long a body has been dead.

I Feel It in My Guts

Microbes live everywhere in and on our body, but the vast majority are in our gut. Many are harmless — think of them as gentle housemates. Some even perform useful tasks like protecting us from disease, making vital vitamins and aiding digestion. Scientists also think our gut bacteria influence health conditions such as diabetes, heart disease and depression.

Did You Know?

There are 700 species of bacteria living on our tongue, gums and teeth. We might think good oral health requires a 'clean' mouth free of bacteria, but it's actually the opposite!

I guess that kind of outdoor microbes wasn't what they had in mind for good digestive health...

I love the great outdoors!

Did You Know?

Studies show that being exposed to outdoor microbes can improve our immune system and reduce allergies, and that spending even a small amount of time in nature can bring benefits.

THE FRENEMY IN ME

Among the trillions of microbes that live inside us is a class of organisms called parasites. They may sound like bad news, but the more we study them, the more we learn that these creatures are in fact both friend and enemy. Frenemies!

What's That?
A **frenemy** is someone whose friendship brings benefits as well as risks.

Is he here again? Why can't he have dinner at his own house?

Well, he IS our daughter's boyfriend after all!

If only his appetite was as small as a microbe!

Did You Know?
Parasites infect other species, called hosts, and live off them. Their name comes from the Greek word *parásitos*, which means "one who eats at the table of another".

One Strange Supper

In 2013, Czech scientist Julius Lukeš sat down to a most unusual meal. A dish of raw fish… crawling with tapeworm larvae. Eww! Lukeš did this to prove that not all parasites are bad for us. He also wanted to learn how certain parasites could help treat human disorders, such as allergies and **inflammation** of the gut. More than a year later, Lukeš said he felt perfectly fine, and had no plans to remove his parasite pals.

What's That?

Inflammation is when a part of the body becomes red, hot and swollen due to infection.

Did You Know?

Lukeš is not the first person to infect himself with parasites. The practice is actually quite common among scientists who study the wriggly creatures, though it is not encouraged because of ethical concerns.

An Ever-Present Problem

Parasites are a problem with a long history, made worse by poor sanitation, dirty drinking water and undercooked food. Intestinal worms and lice have been discovered in ancient toilets, Egyptian mummies and the remains of medieval kings.

Did You Know?
The average human body is home to 400 species of parasites. And that's just the ones we've discovered!

Battle Against the Fiery Serpent

In the ancient texts of Egypt, India and Greece, there are references to "fiery serpents" or "little dragons". Scientists now believe these refer to the guinea worm, a large parasite that travels through human tissue and emerges from ulcers in the victim's feet. The pain is horrific, as if the wound is on fire. Thankfully this terrible disease may soon be a thing of the past.

- When the World Health Organization (WHO) began to fight the problem in 1986, there were 3.5 million cases worldwide, mostly in rural Africa.

- By 2019, the number had shrunk to 54.

- There is no vaccine. But we can prevent the disease by ensuring access to clean drinking water, and filtering water from wells and rivers.

A World Without Parasites?

If parasites cause so much suffering, wouldn't life be better if we got rid of all of them? Tempting, but be careful of what you wish for! Scientists think humans have co-evolved with parasites. For example, without parasites, our immune systems may not develop properly. They say the constant battle between parasite and host forces the two to evolve into more complex species — to outsmart and outwit each other! That's one reason life on Earth is so diverse.

> **Did You Know?**
> Parasites — large and small — are a natural part of a healthy ecosystem. It's estimated that 50 per cent of all the world's organisms are parasites.

The Secret Matchmaker

In the early 1980s, scientists studying the mating displays of North American birds stumbled upon a curious fact. The species that are more prone to blood parasites are also more eye-catching. Their feathers are more colourful, and the males are better singers. But why? Scientists suspect these features are a way to show off that the males had successfully fought off infection. If the females mated with them, their offspring would be equally strong and healthy.

Zombie Ants

Imagine a parasite that not only infects a host, but also takes over its brain and controls its movements. Meet the cordyceps — a fungus that preys on carpenter ants. Infected ants (or hosts) stagger away from their own colony, climb up a tree branch, and die. The parasite then reveals itself, sprouting out of the host's head. To reproduce, it fires spores down towards the forest floor, infecting another carpenter ant.

Worm in Winter, Herb in Summer

One species of cordyceps is actually well known in traditional Chinese medicine. It is called 冬虫夏草 (dōng chóng xià cǎo), which means "worm in winter, herb in summer". Since ancient times, it has been used to treat illnesses like coughs and kidney disease.

Did You Know?
These days, commercial cordyceps is cultivated on rice not insects. Phew!

A Very Unusual Partnership

Flowering plants reproduce through pollination, the transfer of pollen from one flower to another. But the fig tree is unique — its flowers are hidden inside its stem. To reproduce, the plant attracts its pollinator, the fig wasp, to become its parasite!

Hey, There's a Wasp in My Fig!

The fig releases a scent, attracting the female wasp to crawl in. But the hole is so small, she loses her wings. Trapped, she lays her eggs in the seeds while spreading pollen around. Soon, her larvae grow into adults and emerge from the fig carrying pollen, ready to answer the call of another fig tree.

Did You Know?

Wait! So does this mean the crunchy parts of the fig are dead wasps? Fear not! Those are just seeds; the wasp has already been digested by the plant's enzymes.

The Life-Giving Tree

The fig tree doesn't just feed wasps, it also provides food for more than 100 varieties of birds, monkeys, squirrels and elephants. In tropical forests, it is often the only food available for these animals. Due to this, the fig tree is known as a **keystone** species. Without it, the local ecosystem could change or fall apart. And without the parasitic wasp helping to pollinate it, the fig tree would not survive.

What's That?

In architecture, a **keystone** is the stone at the centre of an arch that keeps the whole structure stable and strong. We also use the word to mean the most important part of a system or plan.

WITH A LITTLE HELP FROM MY FRIENDS

Humans have long enlisted the help of animals as warning systems, religious protection and even as medieval healers. In modern times, we study them to solve complex design and engineering problems.

The Wonder Leech

Leech saliva contains a chemical that stops blood from clotting. Since ancient times, people have treated illness by bleeding the patient, and leeches were perfect for the job — their bite was painless, and they could suck up to 10 times their body weight in blood. By the 1980s, leeching was no longer popular, but thanks to American doctor Joseph Upton, leeches continue to be used in surgeries today.

Did You Know?

In 1985, Upton used leeches to treat a boy whose ear had been bitten off by a dog. The reattached ear regained its colour once Upton placed leeches on it.

Did You Know?

A leech has 32 brains, 10 stomachs, three jaws with 100 teeth, and 18 testicles.

Symbol of the Sun

The scarab beetle was a special creature for the ancient Egyptians. It was a symbol of their sun god because it rolled its ball of dung across the ground from east to west. The beetle also represented new life as its offspring would hatch from the dung ball. People would carve stone into scarab designs, inscribe magical spells and wear them as protection.

Did You Know?

Dung beetles are able to roll their dung balls in straight lines, and scientists have discovered how — by using the sun! So what if the sun has set? No problem, the moon becomes their GPS. And when they can't see the moon, they rely on the Milky Way to guide them.

The Sledgehammer Shrimp

The mantis shrimp has a club that packs a pow-pow-powerful punch! It is great for smashing through crab shells, but how does the shrimp protect itself from the impact? The club is made of ceramic fibres and protein molecules, and the answer lies in how they are arranged: in a spiral. This makes the club shock absorbent yet light. Scientists are studying the shrimp for ideas to create stronger and safer structures, like buildings, bridges and airplanes.

The First Pest Busters

In 300 BC in China, citrus farmers cultivated large ants as a defence against caterpillars and beetles that typically infest citrus fruit trees. A special network of bamboo strips was constructed to connect the trees, allowing the ants to scurry across. This was one of the world's earliest forms of pest control.

Swarm Intel

Ants communicate using chemicals called pheromones and behave as one single brain! This special ability is called swarm intelligence. Humans are learning from it in order to build better technologies. Computers that predict the stock market, road navigation apps and self-driving cars — all these are thanks to the tiny ant!

Did You Know?
Other species that display swarm intelligence include migrating birds, spawning salmon and schools of fish.

The Water Conjurer

The Namib Desert beetle lives in an **arid** zone where temperatures hit 45°C (113°F). To survive, it does what few other creatures can — it harvests water from thin air. As the beetle leans its body into the wind, fog accumulates into water droplets on the insect's bumpy surface and rolls down into its mouth. By studying how this works, innovators are developing water harvesting systems for thirsty desert communities. They could even invent a bottle that refills itself using water vapour from the air!

What's That?
An **arid** land or climate has little or no rain.

A Rail Headache

In 1989, Japanese engineer Eiji Nakatsu has a problem. He works for Japan's superfast Shinkansen rail network, and the trains are too loud. They can be heard from 400 m (1,300 ft) away. As a birdwatcher, Nakatsu realises that birds may provide the solutions to the issue:

- The serrated wings of the owl muffle noise, allowing the bird to swoop down on unsuspecting prey.
- The rounded belly of the Adélie penguin lets it slide effortlessly on ice.
- The long beak of the kingfisher allows it to dive into water to catch prey without making a splash.

Nakatsu redesigns the trains, imitating these **aerodynamic** features. The result? Trains that run more smoothly, quickly and quietly.

What's That?

An **aerodynamic** design allows air to pass over an object more easily, so it can go faster.

SHINKANSEN DEPT

Nakatsu-san? The finance department just sent this month's pay for the new design team.

HANEDA'S FRESH FISH

BIRD SEED

Copying from Nature

Observing and learning from animals is one of the ways humans are using nature as inspiration. It's called **biomimicry**. This is the idea that big challenges in design, engineering and **sustainability** have been solved before through 3.8 billion years of evolution. The solutions exist in nature — we just have to find them!

What's That?
Biomimicry is to mimic, or imitate, natural organisms and processes.

What's That?
Sustainability means to take only what we need from the environment to protect it for future generations.

HEROES, ASSEMBLE!

Meet some of nature's superheroes! They are part of the amazing variety of all life on Earth, or what we call biodiversity. With their powers combined, they help to sustain the health of our **ecosystems**.

Did You Know?

We say an ecosystem is a web of life because all the living and non-living things in it are interconnected, like a spider's web. Anything that happens to one part will affect the other.

What's That?

An **ecosystem** is a community of living things and their environment.

ENGINEERS

These are the planners and builders of their environment, maintaining its richness, diversity and health.

Beavers

Superpower: Building dams

Favourite hangout: Freshwater rivers, lakes, streams

We are the busy bees — oops! — eager beavers, who cut down trees, dig canals and build dams. We create a huge impact on the neighbourhood. Our dams keep the waters clean and cool, and prevent soil erosion. They also create flood zones that attract other plants, birds and fish to move in. It's nice to have new neighbours!

Corals

Superpower: Building reefs

Favourite hangout: Oceans, but reef-builders live only in shallow, tropical seas

Our reefs are like big cosmopolitan cities, bustling with all kinds of marine life! Millions of fish, crustaceans, sea turtles, sponges and tiny organisms rely on us for shelter and food, and they love to raise their young in our cosy nooks and crannies. Coral reefs protect coastlines from storms and erosion. They are also a source of income for people who fish there.

Did You Know?

Australia's Great Barrier Reef is the world's largest coral reef system. It is so big, it can be seen from space! But it is under threat due to global warming, pollution and overfishing.

RECYCLERS

Recyclers decompose dead plants and animals and return them to the soil as nutrients for other living plants and creatures.

Earthworms

Superpower: Gobbling dirt and tunnelling

Favourite hangout: Moist soil

Our secret weapon is our gut, which runs the entire length of our bodies. As we gobble up tasty soil, our digestive system breaks it down into nutrients that can be easily absorbed by other plants and organisms. As we wriggle around, we loosen the soil, allowing oxygen and water to reach plant roots, keeping the plants happy and healthy.

Did You Know?

Greek philosopher Aristotle (384–322 BC) called earthworms "intestines of the soil". Centuries later, Charles Darwin (1809–1882), best known for his theory of evolution, would spend 39 years studying these wrigglers.

Did You Know?

The scientific name for earthworms, *Oligochaeta*, means "few bristles". The bristles help the worms stay anchored in the soil as they move.

Fungi and Bacteria

Superpower: Teamwork

Favourite hangout: Plants, trees, soil

We are the Batman and Robin of decomposition, the perfect partnership. Working as a team, we break down dead leaves on the forest floor, each of us processing different chemicals. When our job is done, what's left are carbon dioxide, nitrogen and water: plant food!

Did You Know?

The way fungi and bacteria work with plants and insects can be described as symbiotic. This means everyone gets to benefit.

GARDENERS

Whether it's planting seeds, pruning vegetation or fertilising the ground, it's all in a day's work for these hardworking animals.

Meet Ella! She's the consultant I hired to help us with our memory problems...

Squirrels

Superpower: Forgetfulness

Favourite hangout: Trees

Er... call us accidental superheroes. We love to stock up on nuts and seeds, and we bury them everywhere. However, we sometimes forget where they are! But we're told that it's not a bad thing, because the forgotten nuts and seeds get to grow into new plants and trees, which in turn sustain many other species of wildlife.

Did You Know?

Some consider squirrels pests as they strip and eat bark, damaging young trees. They sometimes also steal food meant for birds. In the UK, the grey squirrel is an **alien invader** that is causing the native red squirrel to become extinct.

What's That?

Alien invaders or **invasive species** are animals that are brought into a new habitat, and which end up causing harm.

Elephants

Superpower: All-in-one gardening service

Favourite hangout: Savannahs, grasslands, forests of Africa and Asia

We know, we're hardly little! In fact, we're like bulldozers, stomping about! But you see, this creates gaps for sunshine to reach plants growing on the forest floor. When we eat, we tear down vegetation from high branches and other species can join in. And when we roam far and wide, we spread seeds — and nutrients — as we, er... poo. We are true ecosystem superstars!

GUARDIANS

Also known as sentinel species, these guardians of our ecology report on the health of our environment. Some can even forecast the future!

Butterflies

Superpower: Reading the pulse of nature

Favourite hangout: Everywhere — tropical forests, deserts, grasslands, tundra

We're more than just beautiful creatures — we can tell you lots about the health of an ecosystem. Our short life cycles mean we are sensitive to even the tiniest changes in the environment. Our larvae are also picky eaters and will suffer if the plants they like disappear. And if we decline, other species are affected too, such as the birds that feed on our caterpillars, and the flowering plants that need pollinators.

Mussels

Superpower: Detecting pollution

Favourite hangout: Coastal rocks

Dump your nasty chemicals into the water? We'll sniff it out. Heavy metals? Can't escape us. We filter seawater to feed on the phytoplankton inside. And if there are pollutants present, we store them in our bodies and make them easy for scientists to detect. All around the world, we help humans monitor pollution in rivers and oceans. Don't mess with us!

Did You Know?

Between 1911 and 1986, canaries were used by miners to detect toxic carbon monoxide inside coal mines. But some felt the practice was inhumane, and canaries were later replaced by electronic detectors.

INSECT APOCALYPSE?

Biodiversity and the health of our ecosystems depend on the health of insects. That's because there are so many of them! Ninety per cent of all animal species are bugs. But bugs are now facing an **unprecedented** threat. And if they are in trouble, so are we.

What's That?
apocalypse:
An extremely destructive event.

What's That?
unprecedented:
Something that has never happened before.

Did You Know?
It's said that at any one moment, there are approximately 10 quintillion insects flying, climbing, hovering, crawling, swimming, marching around us. That's 10,000,000,000,000,000,000!

9,800,263...
9,800,264...
9,800,265...
Eh? Er... Oh!
Nooooo... Sigh...
1, 2, 3...

Poor guy was trying to count ALL the bugs in the world...

He should just count mice. There are only three of us!

What Makes an Insect?

Insects are the planet's most diverse creatures. All adults have three body segments, six legs, antennae and a rigid **exoskeleton**. But that's where the similarities end. Many have wings but some don't, some have scales and some are furry, some have horns while some have fake legs!

Did You Know?

The longest insect known is the giant walking stick from South East Asia. It can grow up to 60 cm (24 in). And the smallest? The fairyfly, barely 1 mm (0.04 in) in length.

What's That?

An **exoskeleton** is a hard external shell that supports and protects the insect.

Little Things That Run Our World

The American biologist Edward Osborne Wilson calls insects "the little things that run the world". Here's why they are so essential:

- Pollinators: Insects help flowering plants by spreading their pollen, a fine powder needed for reproduction. This process allows the plants to make seeds, ensuring their continued survival.

So sorry about your hay fever, but the plants need to survive...

POLLEN

- Food: Insects are a key part of the diet for many fish, birds, reptiles and mammals. This benefits other species further up the food chain that feed on those animals.

Is there a way we can get this guy into the food chain?

Let me call Croc!

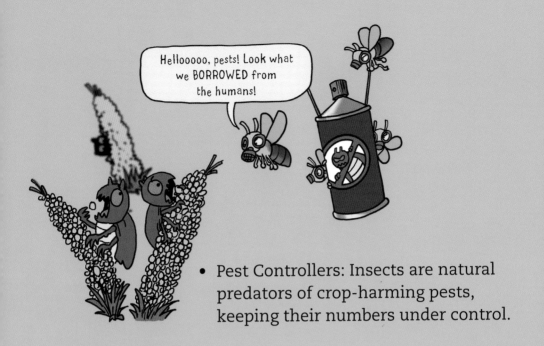

- Pest Controllers: Insects are natural predators of crop-harming pests, keeping their numbers under control.

- Recyclers: Insects break down waste and dead organic matter, recycling precious nutrients back into the soil.

The Perfect Pollinator

Bees are nature's perfect pollinators. Their furry legs and bodies are ideal for collecting sticky pollen, and different species have evolved to suit all kinds of flower shapes. Some bodies are narrow for flowers shaped like tubes, while others are round for flowers that look like bowls. There are even tiny bees that are just right for tiny flowers! Bees pollinate 80 per cent of the world's plants, including most of our favourite food crops, such as apples, cherries and potatoes.

Did You Know?
A single honeybee can pollinate 5,000 flowers a day. A colony visits 2 million flowers to produce a jar's worth of honey. These are truly busy bees!

Did You Know?
Our love of honey goes back a long way. Eight thousand-year-old rock paintings of honey hunting have been found in Spain, while ancient Egyptian doctors made use of honey's antibacterial and antiseptic properties.

CELEBRATE THE BEE!

WOOT!

YAY!

HOORAY!

Where Have the Bees Gone?

But bees are in danger. In 2006, across the US, worker bees suddenly and mysteriously disappeared without a trace. Without the workers, the remaining bees could not feed themselves. This is known as colony collapse disorder. It wipes out 40 per cent of US honeybee colonies each year, contributing to a global decline in bee numbers. But what's worse is that it's not just bees that are disappearing, but all insects.

Did You Know?

Another major killer of honeybees is the varroa mite, a parasite that feeds on the body fat of bees.

Insect Apocalypse

In 2017, insect researchers in Krefeld, Germany, stumbled on a shocking find. The numbers of flying insects, from bees and wasps, to flies, moths and butterflies, have plummeted by 80 per cent in the last 20 years! Newspapers called this "Insect Apocalypse". Soon, **entomologists** in other parts of the world were also reporting steep declines.

What's That?
Entomologists are scientists who study insects.

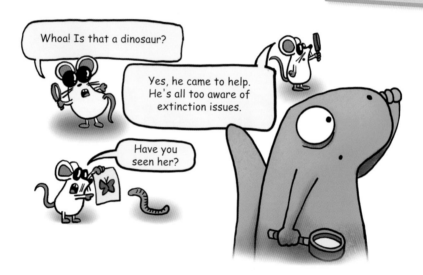

Poisoned Land

Why was this **ominous**? Because insects are extremely resilient. They have adapted to life on Earth for over 400 million years, and have even survived mass **extinction** events. What's causing them to disappear now? One answer is that we're using too much chemical pesticides on our farms. This poisons our landscape, killing not just pests, but other insects and organisms too.

What's That?
ominous: Giving the worrying impression that something bad is going to happen.

What's That?
Extinction is when an entire species dies out.

World Out of Sync

Another danger for insects is *climate change. You see, insects are highly sensitive to the weather. It tells them when to mate, hatch and grow — like an internal clock. This clock is in sync with the life cycles of other living things in their food chain. But climate change is messing up the biological timetable. Over time, this affects the ecosystem.

*See Change Makers: The Earth Experiment

Did You Know?

In some places, warmer temperatures result in pest larvae emerging early, giving them more time to infest food crops.

Did You Know?

Humans also possess an internal biological clock called the circadian rhythm. It's why we feel sleepy at night, and why our mood changes with the seasons.

THE EX-FACTOR

Ninety-nine per cent of all plant and animal species that have ever lived, have died out in the past 500 million years. Extinction is a natural and constant part of Earth's history, but scientists say this is happening at a rate that's hundreds, even thousands, of times faster than before. The causes are complicated, but human activities make things worse.

Going, Going...

The IUCN (International Union for Conservation of Nature) publishes a "Red List" of species under threat. Most of their data is from **biologists** and **conservationists** who monitor species populations over time. When an animal has not been spotted for 50 years, it is considered extinct.

What's That?
Biologists
study living organisms.

What's That?
Conservationists
protect the environment and wildlife.

Dodo and Bramble Cay melomys

Why Biodiversity Matters

With every extinction of a species, there is a loss in biodiversity. Why should we care? Only when there is a wide and diverse variety of species, can an ecosystem cope well with natural disasters, climate change and human activities. When we lose species, our ecosystem becomes weaker. This will affect all life, including ours.

Green Deserts

Healthy soil is literally living soil, teeming with bacteria, amoeba, insects, fungi and earthworms. Without these organisms, we would not have healthy plants and crops. But modern agriculture methods spell trouble for these little heroes. The use of monoculture kills off all life in the soil, creating "green deserts" that are empty of nutrients. Without nature's help to fertilise the land, farmers rely on chemicals to do the job, but this harms the soil even more.

What's That?
monoculture: Growing just one crop on large areas of land.

Did You Know?
As a result of monoculture, out of hundreds of thousands of plant species, just nine crops dominate our farmlands and our diets. The top three are rice, wheat and maize.

Did You Know?
Scientists have found that without soil microbes, plants are less able to survive drought. Their roots are not as deep, and they absorb groundwater less effectively.

Troubled Waters

We depend on the oceans to survive. About 3 billion of us eat fish regularly and this creates jobs for millions of people. But our growing appetite is endangering the health of the oceans.

- We are catching fish faster than they can reproduce. As a result, 90 per cent of fish stocks are at dangerously low levels, affecting our future food supply and livelihoods.

- We harvest only certain types of seafood. This creates an imbalance in the food chain that can erode the ecosystem.

Oh, that's just Bruce doing his bit to address the imbalance in the food chain!

The Grazer and the Coral

Have you met the parrotfish? It is a colourful herbivore that lives in tropical seas, and it uses its beak-like teeth to feed on algae and coral. Without its constant grazing, the algae will grow too quickly and smother the coral reef. And that's what happened in the 1980s and 1990s in the Caribbean, when parrotfish was fished to near-extinction. In that time, half of the area's reefs died.

Did You Know?
The Dominican Republic bans parrotfish harvesting for four months every year. The aim is to give the fish time to recover its numbers, which helps protect coral reefs.

Did You Know?
The parrotfish can't digest hard bits of coral, so it passes them out — as sand! In fact, that's what the white sandy beaches of Hawaii, US, are: parrotfish poop!

*See page 21

Beware the Cuddly Killer

Birds are hard workers that keep our world in balance. They pollinate plants, disperse seeds, control insects, and their beauty and birdsong bring us joy. But birds face a potent enemy, one that comes in a cute and cuddly package: cats! Despite appearances, cats have not lost their wild killer instinct, and each year in the US alone, 2.4 billion birds fall prey to their claws.

Did You Know?

Cats were first domesticated in Egypt 4,000 years ago and were brought around the world by European colonists. These alien invaders have led to the global extinction of 63 species of birds, reptiles and mammals.

Game Changers

In the 20th century, people become more concerned about industrial growth and its effect on human health and biodiversity. They start to demand action to **conserve** nature. One inspiration for this new environmental movement is a 1962 book, *Silent Spring*. Written by biologist Rachel Carson, it explains how the overuse of chemical pesticides is killing insects and other wildlife, and poisoning our land and waters. Another game changer is a single photograph, taken 385,000 km (240,000 mi) in space.

What's That?

To **conserve** the environment is to protect and manage natural ecosystems and their living organisms.

Did You Know?

The World Wide Fund for Nature (WWF) was founded in 1961 to save endangered species from extinction. It is the world's largest conservation organisation with 5 million members.

Postcard from Space

In December 1968, three NASA astronauts were circling the moon when they see Earth through their window. *Quick! Take a picture!* This famous photograph, named "Earthrise", reveals our planet as tiny and fragile. It made people realise that life on Earth is interconnected, and that humans have a responsibility to care for nature and all living things.

Did You Know?

The US space agency, NASA, has recreated the moment Earthrise was shot. Scan this QR code to watch the video.

Scan to
check it out!

THERE'S ALWAYS A THUMB-OVER-LENS PHOTO!

PROPERTY OF NASA

Did You Know?

In 1970, 20 million Americans held the world's first Earth Day. Today, Earth Day is celebrated by a billion people worldwide.

RACE AGAINST TIME

We are at risk of losing the little creatures that add beauty, sound and colour to our lives. Our biodiversity crisis is pushing people to find ways to minimise the negative impact of human activities and to protect nature's little big heroes before time runs out.

A Road Fit for a King

Each year, monarch butterflies undertake a unique **expedition** — a 4,000 km (2,485 mi) marathon flight from North America to central Mexico — to hibernate over winter. But this great migration is threatened by our ever-expanding cities and farms. To fight this, conservationists in the US created the Monarch Highway. Milkweed and wild flowers — which the monarch eats — are planted on land along the Interstate 35 highway, which runs close to the butterflies' route. The hope is that these roadside habitats would support the butterflies' journey and increase their population.

Did You Know?
Twenty years ago, a billion monarch butterflies would make the expedition. The latest count is 56 million.

What's That?
An **expedition** is a journey made for a purpose or reason.

Did You Know?
In the US, streams and ditches along busy roads have become protected spaces for migrating fish.

Hey guys, look! No need to pack food for the journey!

YAY!

MONARCH HIGHWAY 2000 KM
Just follow the milkweed and wildflowers

I still wish we could go by plane...

The Big Butterfly Count

A key part of wildlife conservation is knowing how many of a species there are. So every year in July and August, thousands of people in the UK march into the countryside — to count butterflies! They are part of the world's largest butterfly survey, and their efforts help researchers build a picture of how butterflies are faring. In 2020, 1.4 million butterflies were spotted, the lowest recorded in 11 years.

You can put those away. Use THESE!

They may last longer, but plastic flowers are of no use to butterflies...

Oh...

Did You Know?

You can help butterflies by planting nectar-rich flowering plants in your garden. In temperate countries, bluebells and lavender are the perfect butterfly food. In tropical South East Asia, try ixora and golden dewdrops.

Here Ducky, Ducky

A few times a year, after a rice harvest, farmers in Thailand unleash an army of pest killers onto their fields: ducks! These *ped lai thoong* ("field chasing ducks") gobble snails and weeds, while enriching the fields with their droppings. This means farmers don't need to use chemical fertilisers and pesticides, which can pollute the soil and water. Rearing ducks this way is common in some parts of Asia, and conservationists are hoping to introduce this to other countries.

Did You Know?
This is a type of "regenerative agriculture", which aims to improve soil health by encouraging microbes and organisms to grow.

My Six-Legged Meal

Besides changing how we farm, what about changing what we eat? Industrial-scale animal farms create tonnes of waste that pollute our rivers, lakes and coasts, and kill off life in those habitats. Some say, instead of eating meat, why not try insects? After all, bugs are rich in protein, nutrients and vitamins, and rearing edible critters is far less harmful to the environment and ecosystem. Eating bugs could be one way we can save the world!

A Bug Buffet

Don't say yuck just yet! Did you know that bugs are already on the menu for 2 billion people in 130 countries?

Did You Know?
The consumption of insects as food is called entomophagy.

- Mexicans munch on grasshoppers fried in oil, and seasoned with pepper, lemon and garlic.
- Silkworms, crickets, caterpillars and scorpions are common snacks in parts of China, Thailand and Vietnam.
- The region of Sardinia in Italy is famous for *casu marzu* or "crying cheese", a cheese made from sheep's milk with live maggots.
- Some Native American tribes roast their beetles, others make cicada pies.
- The Sora tribe in India loves red ant eggs. They call the delicacy "ant caviar".

Blinded by the Light

Here's an easy way to help our little friends: switch off the light! Artificial light is a danger to billions of migratory birds as it both attracts and confuses them, leading to fatal collisions.

The light also disrupts the life cycles of insects. Artificial light covers one quarter of Earth's surface and can be hard for birds and insects to avoid, but by dimming our bulbs or switching them off when not in use, we can give our friends a much-needed break.

Did You Know?

Moths 'see' at night using moonlight. But often what they think is the moon, is actually a light bulb. They end up flying round and round the light, and in the end, they die from overheating or exhaustion.

Did You Know?

Glass is also a threat to migratory birds, killing 988 million a year in the US. Some cities like New York City, Toronto and Singapore have guidelines and laws to make buildings more bird-friendly, such as the use of non-reflective glass.

HACKING CONSERVATION

Technology is a powerful tool for conservation. It offers us new ways to study wildlife and educate the public, but it also raises important questions on how we should go about protecting biodiversity.

Shh... Hear That?

If you've ever been in a forest, you'd know that nature makes a lot of noise! Scientists are relying on this natural **cacophony** to locate and monitor endangered species, using super-sensitive acoustic sensors that can pick up the squeak of a bat, the croak of a frog, even the buzz of a bee. Such information gives a fuller picture of species health, so conservationists and lawmakers can decide the best ways to protect the ecosystem.

What's That?
cacophony: A loud mixture of noises.

Did You Know?
Acoustic technology is also used to detect sounds of chainsaws, which helps wildlife rangers prevent the illegal destruction of protected rainforest habitats.

A Bug on Bugs

It's challenging to study endangered bugs because they're hard to get close to. So scientists in New Zealand have built tiny trackers that fit onto insects. These trackers send radar signals to robotic drones following them in real time. Scientists can now gather important data about an insect's habits and habitat — simply by hitching a ride on its back.

Did You Know?
Each tracker is about 3-mm (0.12-in) wide, the size of this dash: —

Conservation by Computer

Wildlife conservation is gaining public support, but it requires money and time. As these resources are limited, which species should we protect first? In 2017, the New Zealand government used a computer **algorithm** to decide, based on four criteria:

- Are they well known to the public?
- Is the rate of decline increasing?
- How endangered are they?
- Can they survive without our help?

Many people disagree with this method. They say humans have a duty to protect all animals. But others say when you prioritise, you achieve better results. What's your view?

What's That?
algorithm: A set of rules given to a computer to make calculations or solve problems.

#native #biodiversity #rocks

Social media is spreading the conservation message to young audiences at unprecedented speed and scale. On popular apps like TikTok, eco-influencers are making and sharing fun videos on biodiversity, soil restoration and mass extinctions. These get hundreds of millions of views within days, and inspire young people to learn more about the issues.

Back from the Dead?

Thanks to progress in DNA technology, reviving an extinct animal is no longer fantasy. But is it a good idea? Here are some ways of thinking about the issue:

- **Ecological importance**: Each animal in an ecosystem has a function. But some are more unique, and when they vanished, their habitats declined dramatically. Reviving these animals could help restore damaged ecosystems.

- **Genetic helping hand**: Human activity is changing the world too quickly for organisms to adapt through natural evolution. Genetic engineering might help some endangered species survive better.

- **Risks**: Genetic modifications could go out of control, resulting in "eco-zombies" and "Franken-species".

Did You Know?

Many zoos work to revive dying species, by breeding them in captivity for release into the wild. Successes include the Polynesian tree snail, which is culturally significant in Polynesia. The snail is also valuable to scientists studying evolution.

MY Ideas ECOSYSTEM

Dear Reader,

We live among an incredible array of little heroes. It is our hope that after reading this book, you will have a better appreciation of the awesome things they do to keep our world going.

Maybe you're now inspired to tell your friends and family. Why not use these pages to sketch out some ideas?

Or perhaps you're itching to investigate what's living in your garden. How about drawing as many bugs, birds and creepy crawlies as you can find, or connect them in a food chain?

A journey of discovery awaits!

Love,

Yeen & Dliew

YEEN'S HANDBOOK TOOLKIT

Big or small, all life on Earth is interconnected. Humans may have made things worse for animals and their habitats, but we also have the power to make things better. In the coming years, what you choose to do will determine the future of our shared home. Here's how you can make a positive difference!

Follow Your Curiosity

Learn about biodiversity and what its loss means to all of us. This book is a great first step, but you can seek out other books and websites for specific topics you're curious about. Plus, nature is a wonderful teacher! There's so much you can gain by being outdoors and observing nature's superheroes in action.

Respect Nature

We share our planet with all other living things,
and that means we must learn how to co-exist.
When you're out in nature, be careful of where
you step and don't disturb native plants and animals.

Spread the Word

As you discover new knowledge, don't keep it inside you.
Share it with others! Maybe you could make a website,
or work with teachers and classmates to create a
pollinator garden in your school.

Choose Your Habits Wisely

From what we eat to how we travel, the choices
we make matter. For instance, cars release polluting
gases that worsen climate change, and climate change
affects wildlife. How about skipping the car and taking
public transport instead? Or if it's not far, walk!

ACKNOWLEDGEMENTS

Lots of Thank Yous to:

Hwee Goh, Change Maker par excellence, for her sharp editorial insights and guidance.

Lydia Leong at Marshall Cavendish, for keeping my writing excesses in check.

All the biologists, conservationists, historians and science communicators who created the deep well of knowledge that this book draws on.

And finally, Pierpaolo Simone, my own superhero.

ABOUT
YEEN AND DAVID

Hoe Yeen Nie is an award-winning documentary filmmaker and journalist who enjoys telling stories that reveal unexpected truths about ourselves and the world we live in. She used to be wary of creepy crawlies, but after delving into their strange and incredible world, she is now learning to appreciate and even love them. Yes, intestinal worms included. Follow her adventures @yeen.writes.

David Liew is a prolific artist and sculptor who has illustrated several bestselling book series. The Change Makers series has especially enabled David to return to his history-educator roots. He also supports fellow authors and illustrators as the Regional Advisor to the Singapore Chapter of the Society of Children's Book Writers and Illustrators.